SEQUENCE

ALSO BY A. F. MORITZ

SEQUENCE
A POEM BY
A. F. MORITZ

ANANSI

This edition published in 2015 by
House of Anansi Press Inc.
110 Spadina Avenue, Suite 801
Toronto, ON, M5V 2K4
Tel. 416-363-4343, Fax 416-363-1017
www.houseofanansi.com

Distributed in Canada by
HarperCollins Canada Ltd.
1995 Markham Road
Scarborough, ON, M1B 5M8
Toll free tel. 1-800-387-0117

Distributed in the United States by
Publishers Group West
1700 Fourth Street
Berkeley, CA, 94710
Toll free tel. 1-800-788-3123

House of Anansi Press is committed to protecting our natural environment. As part of our efforts, the interior of this book is printed on paper made from second-growth forests and is acid-free.

19 18 17 16 15   1 2 3 4 5

Library and Archives Canada Cataloguing in Publication
Moritz, A. F., author
Sequence / A.F. Moritz.
Poems.
Issued in print and electronic formats.
ISBN 978-1-77089-982-7 (bound).—ISBN 978-1-77089-871-4 (pbk.).—
ISBN 978-1-77089-872-1 (pdf)
I. Title
PS8576.O724S465 2015   C811'.54   C2014-908365-3
C2014-908366-1

Library of Congres Control Number: 2014953282

Cover design: Brian Morgan
Cover art: Alain Paiement, *Doubles lunes, (stéréoscopies asynchrones)*, 2012
Text design: Alysia Shewchuk
Typesetting: Brian Morgan

*We acknowledge for their financial support of our publishing program
the Canada Council for the Arts, the Ontario Arts Council, and the Government of
Canada through the Canada Book Fund.*

Printed and bound in Canada

To
Dr. Milutin Drobac,
Dr. Tirone David,
and their teams,
with thanks and admiration

CONTENTS

I

Whenever you stop or slow, restlessness stoops
and drives you. Then going on
you feel your legs again, heavy and stiff with wear —
they used to carry you, now you haul them,
damp logs that flicker with pains. You feel your back
    crumbling
from the blows and slippage of your heels in the sand.

Only the extreme end of day pleases anymore,
when the caravan imposes its halt
after sundown in the music of gradually subsiding purple
and the first stars appear mute over the flat round.
Then tired to death you can fall asleep, and there's pleasure
in knowing your great heaviness
sinking into a greater.

So long we've been travelling across
the sand, heat, and panicking light,

that the journey's motion — slow
rocking of our hips as the feet fall and slip,
the rhythm of the stubborn, elderly
camels and donkeys — the motion of

the journey as night begins to freeze
becomes the rest we thought we longed for. Our motionless
bodies in motionless beds,
the slow ceasing bellows of our sides:

motion of a journey that has reached
a rest it earned or seized,
or in a night without stars or wind
has died. The motion
of a journey that has turned to rest,
that continues in the form of rest.

The poet says the death man fears is only
the death of sleep he dies every night.
But you wake up from the sleep of death
in the middle of every night
and feel you're dying — intolerable fear,
and no one coming. You long
for hated dawn
and to be on the way again.

The other sleep.

It's in the dead
of night only
that you wake up —
in the dark between the stars and the sun,
night exhausted, dawn not yet.

Only then is attention real, godlike. Then it sees
how far it is from being god. It sees
in a darkness blacker than the young night's
beautiful colour, known at last
now in nostalgia. A blackness darker
than light in pure space.

Then you recognize
the journey in which your bed is an evening's pause:
it's the house of this moment
in which the journey is a dream.

You got up and wrote down
in such a dead of night
the beginning of your story,
three lines:

a child sat on the green hillside in sun and shade
and cursed god for the death of the belovèd earth
and felt love in skin, nerves, and hair as the day passed over.

But then it grew clear that this was not the beginning.
And each new night
adding a step toward death, as people say,
brought out of you a preface to your preface of yesterday.
Lines of an earlier tomorrow, dim lines of a moister
    brightness,
a further groping
toward the first spring, deeper in the past, the unspoiled,
a walking of the other direction, taking the road
back the way you came, another step
toward where the dawn begins.

"The music of night," the poet says, "is not
in the stars but in
the darkness there between them."
For the stars, then, the dark is their desert
as the blinding desert is the dark for the traveller
who pitches his rag of tatters on the sand
and seems to freeze in place for the night
and with the returning light
go on again. "If man,"
the poet says, "is dust, this thing
that walks through the dry expanse
is a man."

The splendour, painful dazzle, and monotony of the desert.
Always equal. A day of walking, a month, discloses
nothing new and nothing old.
When you were a child under the trees,
one footstep brought you to a fresh world,
newly born, drenched in memory.

Now, no advance from where the last step was planted.
Sand, the ruin of soil. The next place is the same. That instant
when the heel struck and sunk far back there, a yard ago,
already glowed with every brilliance of earth
and our whole futility.

The sky and sun were unveiled there once and for all:
blue and gold: their true bodies, their true names.

With morning, all the labour and pain to come,
all the fading dead,
nevertheless you had a taste for the new day.

You had lived that morning before
in a deep valley outside of time.

There the walls that blocked us in
were forest and stony wooded ridge with threads of cascade,
not openness to a circular horizon over low dunes.

There a river came from and went to unknown places
and brought fish, frogs and turtles, birds, lilies and arrowroot,
rhythm and melody. Trees. Willows overhanging
shelves of the banks for children to be shaded
watching trout and sunfish drift through the water grass.

The caravans of the merchants, Valente writes,
Las caravanas de los mercaderes,
and I wonder, look up in wonder at the street.
And does it matter that the merchant's caravans
are trucks? Huge tractors — Freightliner, Peterbilt,
International, Western Star — and giant cartons
with lettuces and cornucopias of loaves
painted two stories high along their sides.
Big-screen stills from a movie of abundance,
signs of the wealth being
hauled to us, threatening to fall over, to crush us
like a comber, a leaning wall, as the truck strains
to bend around a right-angle corner
and we step back. And think of Anaïs Nin
all at once knowing herself woman, small,
as she walked next to passing truck tires
twice her height. Of Juan Ramón: in childhood
he saw three oxen taller at the shoulder
than the highest roof tiles of the village. Giant
oxen of life and vision: this world is another.
I think of a boy in Babylon lying on his bed,
calm but vibrating in aftermath pleasure,
just having come from his friends, their jokes,
their easy strength. Never again, he thinks
in exultation, will a moment be like ours:
this style of grace, the subtle transformations
ours alone in this incomparable language
that we make with every expedition for love
with the girls, our happy prodding, their happy

defiance. A moment supreme till time ends.
A moment of a world, our youth, our invention,
constant, condensed in a song, and always
living in a next moment, another day. Never
was there in the world nor will there be
this agile splendour and flow. He swells
(as our saying goes) with pride, and looking up
at the cars, backpacks, cellphones, and the trucks
of the merchants, I agree with him, I am him.

When the heel strikes the sand, a chasm opens in thought:
why not stay here and mine for water?
For the spring of this dryness. The hidden or unreal
moisture that you feel here
gathering to pour from its absence into the blindingness.

When the same heel strikes, a thirst arises to go on,
to find the spring anywhere out of here.
A sense of new strength arises:
now as your gaze travels far ahead of you into bluish dust,
this time you won't forget, this time you'll keep
the place and the promise.

II

The desert releases you from thought.

You took one book, not even in your hand,
in memory,
to remind you of what you are:
not a lizard or a dock.

What you are can't be allowed to fade with the stars at dawn
low over the earth
into the rising brightness.
Or be lost in their brightening later in the mantle
of consoling darkness
when slowly it's woven deeper and deeper.

That would be more than a human being deserves.
Too much like a happy death.

The book will remind you
you must care for tomorrow
and you must not care for tomorrow
if you are to live,
and you must live.

The stars have three faces, or vouchsafe three troublings.

The first grace: they're a map above the trackless,
though maybe a map of a way among themselves only,
through the world they are, the one above,
but in this world no map.

The second: they seem like former beasts and heroes,
points remaining from vanished plots.
They remind us of crumbs of stories we own,
can't understand, and sometimes sing,
changing them to make a meagre sense.

The third: as night grows, no one listening anymore, everyone
    sleeping,
map and song fall away and the stars are silent light.

We've fallen asleep. The stars are silent light,
nothing to us, no longer being seen.

But is there this rest from knowing?
It seems you never stop dreaming
and the stars are only damped
the way the sky is for a man in his tent:
the day turns
as always
slowly around
into a different hope and horror coming
beyond the dream, the pitched
and pierced wall.

With darkness we used to stop and retire to prayers.
By custom. And because the desert became frigid.
And each footstep at night expected a crevasse. Knowledge
that the dust was continuous and flat
brought no assurance.

It was hard to believe these prayers said with boredom
were the heart of the day, more living than all the steps
    we'd taken,
the animals and companions who'd fallen dead,
the flight from the oasis
we'd found withered and occupied by lepers.

The only life our prayers had, like our dreams,
was that dead day. Psalms nothing but images of dry trees
and the bones' remembrance of plodding
and the muscles' remembrance of buryings in sand.

O the magnificence of the book,
greater than the stars!

The book is the glory of the stars
as the revealing of God is God's glory,
as a woman or man is the glory of all others

even on the desert
in the pauses of looking up from the book
and seeing

you are here

without a god,
without a man or a woman
to reveal the good,
without another
for you to be the glory of.

Who traced a finger through the night,
zone of black sand, that Tenerife up there,
some explosion's remainder
stretched out silent — drew a finger along,
the way a lover scribbles a name on a beach?
The advancing cursive turned over grains and pebbles.
Some shifted to new angles
and lit up, glinting in straggles, reflecting
a sun I can't see, tracing the loops
of the name it seems was never completed
or the weather spoiled it, stretched and blurred.

Do my steps that kick up yellow dust
and bare some chips of crystal
so that here and there in the dull extent
they shine in their colour of water,
noon-dazzle off water, stars of water
the size of crumbs, hard and few, fallen
from a poor table, a constellation on the floor,
the sign of a goddess, bits of a lost name,
a story forgotten, a new one made up,
a scatter of points to read like words — do my steps
translate the movement of that finger?

We set out because we were commanded
and yet of course we were told equally to stay home.

What curse was it
that our bodies were made to resemble permanence
hour by hour, while our constant nervous
travelling gives the only flesh it has
to passing, the figure of this world?

Our talk loves to turn these few things we know clearly
into unanswered questions
pronounced in a tone of complaint and desire:

these can echo in space and are a song of sorts,
a work song, so a consolation,
a voice that goes with us.

You began to notice that you loved to lie raging at night
till it seemed your head would crack like the egg of a vulture
	of anger
and the chick that came out would be that same crying
	and begging
restored to youth — Come and help me, come at least and say.

You'd find yourself believing you had never slept
and yet you were waking up,
the dew warming on the blanket in the slant sun,
the stirrings, murmurs, of women and men
rising around you, no longer shadowy dwarf bulks.

This was life, how it went. How beautiful it was.

Between the prayer, rage and fear, and dawn,
there must have come a space of silent blackness.

We start at dawn, when the stars fade, on the route planned
according to their pattern last night.

Last night we looked at them and saw how far we'd
    gone wrong
travelling yesterday through their invisibility and the dust.
Last night we understood how unclear — incomprehensible —
had been our readings of the previous night.

Today will be the same. First a course set in darkness.
Then in the bleaching day a wandering from it.
Then night again, and a wondering at that course we chose
    and stumbled on
and a correction for the day to come
by the stars of the new night.

They were crossing a desolation unrelieved
except by the nails
of stars in the frigid night
and the cracking of stones in the sun like gunshots.

No right exists for them to say this.
This is lush Ontario
and their sorrows and longings are mild

although they die in them as much as others die
in borderless dryness.

Commedia without an end, without ends,
no heaven, no hell,
hell and heaven at each point,
each point the purgatory of their conflict,
sun on stone, splendour and its senselessness,
the marriage bed of yes and no.

Unrepeatable sense of the stone,
hard, the stone's secret, plain as day.

Dark as night.

The desert is desert, the meadow is meadow,
whether despair or happiness walks through them.

Despair saps the trees and grass
while they remain where they are in splendour.
Exultation gets up from boredom
to fetch water — the fetch becomes water.

But let the word be only truth.

Sitting on the stairs
staring through the open door
into the maple summer
and the never-learnt
library of stars,
they saw their pain or place
was a desert with its wanderer,
its file or caravan
of adventurers dying
one by one on the way
to a place they'd heard
spoken of. One
had spoken, many listened,
many denied
it was a place, in or beyond
the expanse. It was just a path
that was no path
except that in the trackless
they looked back
to wherever blindly
they had gone. It was a dream
of any sorrow,
every fear,
in any, in every bed.

From those pinpoint
boredoms, men and women,
the brilliant vast
boredom of the desert
radiated into the night,
strange even to them
long dying there:
it seemed always
more strange, each second,
flickering as if
to relapse into
the mass of the wax
the closer death came.

And so they lived
in the idea of the journey
and the path, and doubt
and scorn of the idea.

Our daily bread:
breath, and space
for the progress
of our steps, a world
to be the place,
fields and clouds
around the path
that comes to be
where our steps go.

III

In the mirages of silver
as I drive the late-summer
country roads, lakes of dazzle
on the sun-absorbing and
refusing asphalt
in the rich, well-watered land,
my home, the roads
my only desert and my way
into the thickets and clearings
of this beauty, as I pass by
the aisles of willows
along streams, the woodlots
of the prosperous farms, my car
engulfed in shade
in a long tree tunnel
of maples, with the white
clover perfume
blowing in the windows,
between the tiger lilies of the ditches
and sweet pea and faintly violet
convolvulus twining
on wooden fence posts
and black fence wires,
the brown and white of six
couched Holsteins, two black
horses grazing motionless
far away, and the spray of golden
mustard flowers on the slope
where Father took me to chase
butterflies, I remember
the end of my house.

The hooves hollow on the parched August ground
that night beyond the walls. What was it
out there, approaching? We crept down
from the bedrooms, my mother, father, and I,
moved toward the window, but first the door
broke open, four men ran in. My uncles,
my mother's brothers. They took her screaming,
took me screaming, shot Father. We were tied struggling
in heavy ropes, gagged, loaded on the flat low-sided wagon,
and carted like pigs of iron or sacks of lettuces.
Two uncles rode before, two behind, their rifles
butted on their thighs, muzzles high, and their men
on each side with the torches they'd brought to the house,
torches put out now, to pass along invisible
as our procession entered the silent town.

So now the Howes had her back, as they'd always sworn,
from Liberatore, the filthy Catholic, the filthy farmer.
For six years I'd lived happily in the meadows, stream banks,
woods, and fields. The world sparkled, the nights were kind
and filled me with eagerness for the new day. The only dark
was a child's faint awareness of the other family in the town,
never visited, scarcely ever seen. Sometimes we'd go past
their offices, a cube of brick, in the town they'd named
for themselves, or see their mill on the creek bank
back of the row of stores, and Mother would repeat
that these belonged to her family, and name her father,
who'd been her friend. I'd seen the squat church
with a low crenellated tower, where they were founders
        and elders.

I remember an ancient silo clad in tile,
white once, now brown, like an old man's teeth,
and covered in vines. We had passed it in our wagon,
Father and me, on who knows what never-repeated errand,
and I had no notion where it was but I always
remembered it. In my child-mind's map, which lacked
all exact location but in mysteries corresponded
exactly to that land, the tower stood forever,
an enchanted monument of a splendour
fallen long ago, somewhere in the world around us.
The Howes had been like that to me, strange fires somewhere,
strange shapes of mute blackened buildings, until that night
when I was dragged to live with them and be their son.

They were the law there. As soon as I heard and got
this idea, law, I thought that law had been the fields,
when I was small, and the seasons, and Fr. DeVrie
coming out a long way to bless them
in the midst of planting time in the name of the Madonna.
A May altar with the mother and child clay statue, with
   lilac sprigs
and lilies and lilies of the valley from our yard
and kitchen garden, where Father had a way
of ranking the vegetables in rows behind each other,
a secret way, his own, so that the rabbits were discouraged.

Bring flowers of the fairest . . .

From garden and woodland and hillside and vale . . .

The law then was Father on his wagon, sometimes me
   beside him,
coming back from the farther fields with wheat,
at other seasons turnips, or potatoes, which were new then:
I remember the excitement of the new crop.
I remember the bean flowers and twining sweet pea.

O Mary, we crown thee with blossoms . . .

                                        All this
had been the law, so now I saw things newly: law
and then another law that drives the first one out,
the succession of laws, which is history,
which is forgetting and decay.

September the wandering workers used to come,
and Father would hire his three to help bring in
wheat, oats, and barley, and finish the hay.

Evenings, Mother and the other women rode out from town
and at trestle tables fed all the hands hired
by the farms round about. Then the men slept in the barns.

Two weeks of heaven, more heaven still than the others.
The strange workmen, skin dark and marled
as river stones, speaking purling tongues, their bodies

knotted and small, almost as small as mine,
but tireless, powerful, like gnomes and trolls.
From far away, to see Father with them out in the fields.

The crystalline sky enclosing. A cloud passes across,
Father bows his face to the earth and around us
in the circle the shy distant meadowlarks and bluebirds,

dragonflies by the muddy banks, their belovèd home,
orioles in the top of the hornbeams dividing the meadows,
grey kingbirds I'd meet on fragrant paths in the woods.

Mother was uncontrollable.
They shut her in. So she closed herself in her room,
except to plant and tend some flowers, closely watched,
around the back door, near where the water pump
stood on a small porch with woven open-work walls,
green-painted — I remember her lilac bush,
like the one there'd been by the back door of our house.
After five years of this she died, in my eleventh,
and became a memory, more in my body than in my mind:
her care for a child, succour as they call it, and then
five clear years of rages sinking into ghostliness.
The same June, sex rose in me.

I had been made a Howe
and silently I hated everything. Except my wandering,
which gradually resumed as they came to trust me,
or rather, ignore. The useless boy with books,
who went back to them soon after any barrage
of shouts and kicks. The one who did what he was told,
did all his homework, got his A's, without a word,
without a sign of desire or resentment.

But by the stream again, at last, under the willows and oaks,
watching the water lilies and the bass slipping between them,
the flights of goldfinches and grasshoppers,
finding the small snake and the mantis, stopping to read
in a hut-sized hall of green the brush
had woven of itself in the woods, friends with the tanager
    and bluejay . . .

there was no denying the ancient delight
of my skin, my sight, my smell and hearing. I could not
    understand
the way the birds, the thick green, and the light of the sky
mixed in me — or did not mix, merely dwelt, merely abided —
side by side with the broken stones of the Howes' old mill race
from the patriarch Daniel's time, when the one furnace
turned out a poor ton of spongy iron a day —
and side by side, too, with the might of the new factory.
I'd sit by the creek and look up at it on the opposite bank,
long, high, black, at night sending a blue-orange glow into
    the dark.
While the crickets and cicadas chirred in my ears, I'd stare

and feel pride, knowing it was mine, it could be mine,
and I could go within there whenever I wanted,
had often been there, watching, a chosen son,
as the ladle tipped molten steel into the moulds
and the men, heavy-booted and visored, stood back from
    the sparks.

Father hadn't been killed. He recovered and lived
a shadow life, impotent of justice, out there in the beauty
where the shaded house backed on the stream, and Mother's
lilac continued to bloom. I took to visiting him
in the freedom of the ever-deepening indifference
around me. I'd walk out along the creek bank
or later along the rails, then cut across the fields.
How strange to walk the railway: the ugly backs of buildings,
then out into the open, the blue and grey slag underfoot,
flying grasshoppers rising, unfolding their black and gold,
and to each side the wild wheat, ironweed, milkweed,
        tiger lily,
as your eye squints from the dazzle off the polished rails
and you struggle to fit your steps to the narrow, slightly
        uneven
rhythm of the ties. Father still drove his wagon to his farther
        fields,
sometimes I'd sit by him again, help load and unload,
there were neighbours now and he'd hand them out
cabbages, carrots, beans. In the evening he'd play
an Italian song on the Jew's harp, then maybe sing it softly:
I didn't know a word. In the fall he'd have one cow butchered
and take the hide to be cured, and make his own shoes
        from it
out in the shed. Everything as it had been. Then one day
the Howes' police chief came and said he'd hanged himself.

What would it be to take a sufficient revenge,
to burn everything? To walk away from the flaming town
in the music of the screams, out into the desert
the heat has made of the earth. And is it a fool's game,
a coward's, to burn it down in words? — words
that can't help bringing human and divine
wisdom with them, since they're partly made of those,
and so they prevent the burning, except in fugitive images,
because the just must not suffer with the unjust.

For thirty years I never went back.
By then the town was empty,
the Howes my uncles had died, the family
had vanished into a few teachers and waitresses
with other names, names of humble husbands.
The headquarters building, mainly empty,
housed one tattoo parlour in the south corner
fronting the street, next to the white brick
Catholic church and the stained glass window
Father had donated, Christ welcoming the children.
The cement approaches to the main factory
were cracked by flowering weeds, chicory,
and tall dandelions, the hangar doors
sagged open, mourning doves sheltered
and cooed inside.

I drove out to the farm.
Left the car by the long drive, a short road really,
through the near field, the house's grove,
and the wide yard. Walking up I passed
under the hanging tree: the old oak
alone on the lawn, now gone wild,
in front of the porch. I saw that where he'd hung,
underneath, there was a sour yellow circle
where nothing grew, a circle of white and damp
short grass that seemed to have sprung and died
and matted together and rotted all at once.

So I stood in the circle. First the cicadas
chirred around me, and beyond the oak shade
the green tips of the young wheat sparkled blue
and waves of breezes ran across them. Then I heard
a faint crying. Was it words, or just a sound,
a man whimpering? Sobs. Disconnected gulps.
Sometimes it seemed the sounds were saying, "Help me,
help me." And then they disappeared. Or was it
that I stepped back terrified, out of their world,
onto the good green clover? I paused there
for my breath to start, and stepped forward again.
The paintless house with its broken windows
and door sagging open, with the treetops
along the stream shining behind it,
and in the circle the faint voice came again,
as long as I stood there it came, wordless,
sometimes like "Help me," sometimes maybe
a phrase in my lost Italian.

IV

When time will be restored, I said,

time the procession of our pleasure,
which has to proceed to be,

time the unforeseen
advent of new pleasure,

when time will be wholly a coming once again,
will move toward us and enter us,

will always be coming there

from past, future, and all directions,

will be nothing else,

forever arriving,

coming into where we stand, walk, and lie.

If god is dead
and lies in the earth,
mouth and eyes in the wet cramped roots,
contours pressed at every point by mud,
as far as possible from the freedom that is god,

the body without body

whose movement is so agile
it possesses without moving
every space and time,

are we wrong, are we guilty
to be crushed at what has happened to that body
that was
to be ours,
and the promise it gave us, or seemed to,
the promise that maybe we only heard?

Maybe our being crushed, scattered, and disappointed
is the true death, the one god needs to die.

That we are blind to see
any transformation ever coming again
may be the deep earth
in which god's corpse needs to lie.

Of course one who does not see what can't be seen
but needs to be
is always wrong and guilty.

If god is dead
and lies in the earth
until the earth passes

and then lies nowhere.

After the last passing
of all the passings
of winter into spring, harvest, and winter.

The last passing of these images
on the plain of waiting and looking
for what was imagined.

The last spreading of the desert
and lengthening of the night
and outpouring of the mouth of dreams.

The freedom that is god, I said.
The body without body

whose movement is so agile
it possesses without moving
every space and time.

But the prophet I remember
said the opposite:

"Freedom,
for which fire became man."

What did you go out into the desert to see?

Of course what I've always been going to see:
the perfect man
emerging into visibility,
merging into my own body
at the end of my progress

though what I'm nearing
is a hundred years and a widening of the tract of sand.
But this is an image, this tract. I mean I fear
in the place I'm nearing, dark and light are one
but not as when I was a child
in the shade under the tree.

The sufficient illusion that is childhood,
and the sufficient illusion
that childhood had.

One is built on the other and then the other
is built out of the first again
perpetually. At this point the building
becomes, returns to
being growing.

And the one who lives in the secret
abides in the shade.

And the sufficient illusion
childhood is.

You heard a murmuring like a stream,
its voice growing as someone approaches it in the woods.

Treasure carefully in mind the highway
by which you went. Return.

The whole valley of the dead bodies and the ashes
will be sacred. The city
will be built again on its mound.

The children will come back, will be
as they were of old, your work
will be paid, you'll see
the grace you found in the desert,
an everlasting love. You have a future,
the children will come back,
your child will return. Return.

The babble of a stream like a prophet singing
where he thinks that there is no one.

To be grateful to time, the mercy
of eternity, and to your bones,
their beautiful concert. Without these the moment is ice.
Thanks to the bones' complicity with time,
you can move on to one more summer
and you can move back into resenting them.

You can fall into resenting them
and feel that resentment is
to be frozen there
and know that this is an image.

In the stillness imagined there's motion
as there is motion even in ice hardening toward deeper winter.

This crevice between fixed idea and moving body
sharpens the blood they share.

And so you arrive
not at gratitude, only the reason to be grateful,
reason for the moment hated,

and begin to think of moving on.

The darkness seems
to hold the stars still
clenched in its immobile distance.
The lights of the stars are like the sight of human eyes:
they push into the black, never piercing, pressing to
    move across,
to make it a bridge delivering the feet
to the starting place tomorrow.

But they never cross it. Frozen
in place, bits of ancient story,
like bone ends of utterly forgotten beasts
poking through the sand. As these the stars come
motionless and silent to our eyes but later
have shifted westward and later
are gone. There has been sequence, music
through the dark carrying the crumbs that remain,
making sound, silent
sound of the unreadable
idea.

And so: patience, it seems, until
and after death, in every breath in sleep
and every footstep when morning melts
the resolve of night
never to move again.

In the evening
when the shape of the leaves is insanity,
their tremor, their hanging, their colour, lost,
and darkness, the loved relief, comes as hollowness,
the heart devises the desire
to go out never turning back and chew the dust.

In the evening.
In the elderly brittleness of the last letter that ever came
     from her
on the stained unlighted table.
In the heat of the soles of the feet
in the plod of chores around the walls,
creak of the winch, shoulder-wrecking slosh of the water
     and slop,
flurry and cackle no human hears or sees.
Work so that the being can live until it dies.

That's when the heart receives the idea of the desert.

If you ever stop or slow, restlessness comes and drives you.

You thought you had achieved a house
and a plot of flowers and food plants, animals and birds
    around it.
There thought would halt and gaze out the window.
There sleep would always come with dark and waking
    with light.
The ancient and proper rhythm.
Dreams and memories would be the constellations,
hope the sun, and the blood of man the sunlight.

But restlessness comes. It regathers in you.
You saw yourself, a fly battering the panes,
a nervous motion in black leaves,
a breeze or ghost circulating in the garden paths
without rhythm, like a lost or crazy blood.

If you ever stop or slow, restlessness comes and drives you.

The householder abandons the belovèd house,
not even closing the door,
scarcely glimpsing in an instant's image
the garden in future merging into the wild.

You know now you'd wander even if shut up in an atom.

The compulsion is to the longest paths, the unbordered.
The house diminishes, now it's a ship you once hailed
     for rescue
and it passed by unseeing, maybe empty and adrift,
till it became a dot, then nothing.

On the horizon to which you had turned your back.

She and I climbed through the level
summits of our neighbourhood.
An ascent of pleasure. The steepest
verticals there we took with the lazy
ease of atomies drifting up
a waterfall of light. Floating back
upstream in the new warmth:
the spring had come, all-powerful
soft current, spreading
from its centre everywhere.
We talked. The belovèd
foreign streets and images
we had stayed in, had stood before
nine months ago: their names were
being forgotten in us now, but the casement
of our window there, and the courtyard
at the hotel, a triangle glowing emerald
a hundred feet below us,
and the impasto of the Madonna,
the rabbit under the feather spray
of her hand's gesture,
burned in our words. Recalling,
almost dreaming. Here in our eyes
the short season of the magnolia
already was letting fall
its fleshy shame. Two days' burning
rose and white — an adolescence
reduced to a blinding spark,
a quick leap from childhood
into the long middle — a leap

so brief, so bright, it almost blinds
with tears. A wind shook
the tree, its chalices, its stars, decaying
flowers open freshly above us,
and threw more browning
petals down. For a moment
we were that wind. It took our bodies,
glad to be visible, to walk, see, talk,
be two together and almost still.

They walked and walked
and as they walked
they sang "Eternal
Memory" and the psalm
"The earth is the Lord's
with all that is in it,"
and when they stopped
the walk and the singing
went on in their nerves
and muscles, in
the hushed animals,
cab horses, shivering
street-corner dogs
that stirred and sighed
with stumbling breath,
in the wind that kept
the rhythm in its rise
and fall, its faint
buffeting around
sharp buildings . . . the walking
of the wind that seemed
to slow almost to
nothing toward dawn.
And so they learned. They walked
through the world, the city, and
other times they stopped
waiting.

She said,

We are so happy right now
let's say a prayer asking for nothing.

Maybe you should have stayed here
where you began.
Who knows?
Maybe you were right to go on.

Maybe you don't believe there's any question
and you ask as a way of pretending you're innocent
of freedom stolen
by not seeing what is clear.

Who knows?

You had nothing to live for there. Only life.

Was there a spouse and children? You can't remember
if you betrayed anything but emptiness.

A house. Streets and houses. Neighbours. A store.
There you sat among piles of rugs, bolts of stuff,
tureens, stacks of plates and cups, sets of silver,
foxed linens lying unsold since your father's day,
with your old cashier behind you, your brother, the
    unsuccessful one.

Probably a dream. What others had,
the old folks, never you. A former world
that rested breathing under the light of its star.

You had nothing to live for there.
That's your excuse.

What did you come out into the desert to see?

The paradise that was lost in me.

But what did you come out into the desert to see?

The flowering forest, the hillside, the stream.
The cat that stayed beside me, purring, in my waking dream.
The fountain of my blasphemy.
When I was soft and supple
and almost as small as a cat.
Alone in the pre-dawn,
a child, slipping away,
all the house behind me sleeping.

But what did you come out into the desert to see?

I did not come out to see, only to hear
the music of glory, the human more than human,
and the crowd noise of judgement lost in the silence of mercy.

The noise of the crowd that has somehow come within
my own innocent ear.

The desert is produced
by your footsteps.
If you weren't wandering
it would not be desert.

Imagine stopping someday.
All at once the sand flowers.
A house springs up
waiting for you, a house
that never existed until now,
that you have never dreamed,
and yet a house you built
long ago. And a house means
a village, even if distant,
so a village is there.

But the sand doesn't flower.
You simply see
it always was a garden
around the house
that is there, was always,
that you never built,
that you started from.

The wandering came later.
Now, living here
in the house you've found,
you try to see
even though it came later
it was the seed.

VI

Still another retelling of the tale from a minor player's part,
a cliché, a wish, said Ulysses standing there
laughing at me.

And Elpenor was there too, dithering
some steps behind him in the dusty nervous shadows,
picking his teeth with a nail he'd let grow too long
and looking back and forth it almost seemed in dread.
His motions were the loosening of a leaf in a small wind,
like someone who tenses his hand for a quick clutch
he doesn't believe in
to catch a fly. Was he human anymore,
wasn't he just a brain ruined by too much sun at the beach?

Ulysses by contrast was massy and broad-chested,
and his old brown teeth veined with remnant streaks of white
blocked me — that closed smile with the amber eyes
glistering above, a sunset that still can blind — blocked me
like a city gate closed at night. A brilliant
smile. A blank.

Elpenor on the other hand would never be old.
What did his viewpoint matter,
his injustices, his slaveries, his slovenliness,
his doglike following along, his little angers,
murmurs of protest, gone like children's?
He gave a snort.

And Circe was there too. Where
is your island, Circe — your sea, your realm,
where you are queen, witch, and rumour
until crossed by a history? Gone. Now
you're a woman of the camp. The camp that is nothing
with its quibbles and their rebel leaders:
tussles under a blanket.

And so, Ulysses,
if we don't and can't erase the kings,
if we're not all kings,
we're nothing?

A smile:
a wall. He was gone.
An old man, stinking, with a wire buggy full of papers,
a chuckle or sob from around a brick corner —
brick: the old part of town.

To be on the road: another imitation,
another cliché, like everything humans do.
We like the idea that a cliché turned slightly
is an archetype: a cliché looked at "in a new light,"
maybe the light of the desert. We like evasions.

The lonely public road. No one escapes it.
Everyone's here. Some plainly crazy,
shouting, rushing, reversing, like massive midges
weaving a never-formed tapestry of ugly knots.
Some driven out of yet another country,
infested mattresses on the roofs and children
looking from windows of 1957 station wagons
that have to be pushed along, rusted Rosinantes.
Some in the robes or nudities of various faiths.

The lonely public road,
the path to the spring in the forest,
the trudge through the trackless waste,
the most crowded place on earth.

What did you come out into the desert to see?

Certainly not someone howling at me,
all my faults, just like back in the city,
someone in an urban fast-food joint
dressed like a prophet,
or a relentless traveller, Ulysses
or Ahasuerus, condemned to wander,
belt of rope, meal of crusts, rinds, and melted ice
rescued from plastic bags in cubic bins,
scrotum lolling out of gapped and sagging pants,
stink of sweat and urine. Although out here
the smell is scoured away
by the perpetual stinging bath of wind-driven sand
and at night the sharper faster particles
of the stars.

I am a modern man,
this that goes along in the guise of a member of a salt-route
    caravan.
Or in the guise of not even a man at all,
a mollusc from when this desert was a sea
that insists with its creeping that its world remains
somewhere in the dry air.

I'm a modern man and insist on the body.
All transfiguration comes in the body
and partakes of sickness, the itch, the wash of crying
    chemicals,
the world's flesh-eating schedules, the steps of sunset.
Of needing to endure the unendurable separation.
Struggling to wake again bright every moment in this bed.

But I feel my face and see the dunes:
low heaps with lax slopes
like cheeks, jowls, and forehead sifting away.
So don't tell me the bones are not a jail for the spirit.
I'll die in these bones that will remain unchanged
even when they're nothing. I am an ancient man.

The stone split in the noon, the grey black stone.
With a gunshot crack it split in the slow shush-shush
of our soles on the sand, the rhythm of a wire brush
as the timekeeper nods off behind the sleeping band
and night advances through blue lights, sweet smoke,
　　empty glass.

And the stone was not and is not penetrated by the sun.
As soon as our eyes flew to the source of the sound
it was lying there, two stones, two worlds of dark inside.

Destroyed and healed in one instant, annihilated
in others without pain. After having burned
an eon in the maddening panicking sun
without desperation or fear. We longed to be stone.

We yearned for the superiority
the man who knows one thing
feels toward the man who knows two.
Yearned for the greatest proximity
possible for humans to stone.
We yearned with the everlasting
arrogance of eminent persons
who believe from above they see.

We yearned to forget
back to the seed. To leave behind
all it had been to grow up.
Yearned to be triturated like the rock,
split and split and split
into crystal flakes
that never wounded give
a body, always new bodies
to transparency. Yearned to be
innumerable bodies and in the wind
the smoke of dust
driven through the light
or if the light and wind
had died by then, then still in the dark.

We yearned to grow down and back
to the child. We called the child
fruit, flower, and reason of the human.
We said the long afterward, our life . . . we possess it merely
so that the child at its beginning can be:

the aching care for the child
to give it its paradise, trying to last for that task,
the care to contradict the withering of our muscles,
the falling apart of our bones, falling asleep
of our nerves, our needs, their glamour — this struggle
     only exists
because it must for the child, its beginning, to be.

We said, "I have had my paradise."

Evil dreams. The child a wanderer through
the desert of them
into ruined adolescence, the last garden.

The voice of the prophet came to us like the squeaking
of a bat receding in the night:
I am more than eighty years old . . .
what bloom is this more than the bloom of youth . . .
beauty that descends on me and rises out of me . . .
O if I could only return to the house where I was born

and hear the birds, the same birds
that were my friends then, sing once more.

We heard the voice rustling, remembered only now, in the ear
of our childhood's end: Woe to you
who are rich,
you have had your consolation.

VII

We came to a city of slim cones. Narrow structures
higher than steeples, dwindling to needle points.
The winds whined and wavered in them, making a harp.

They were covered with dust as though ancient.
We rubbed and it fell and we thought
the material would soon appear: brick, chromium, glass . . .
But it never appeared. As long as we worked, more dust.

Each tip was pointed to one of the stars, said someone.
After a few days, the sun dazzle drove us out.
It was less than in the open desert but there it made the
    shadows,
the sundial maze of the shadows.

You had nothing to live for there.
Only life. But where is there that life can't be sung
and what other task of life exists but singing?

There's the hard labour
sometimes to live, sometimes torn or made to sag away
    from life,
hard labour for nothing.
And there's what lies at the edges of labour,
the inconsequential and the useless:

the centre:

the fountain that saves and fails in the maddening sun:

the chained prisoner along the roadside
hears the meadowlark out in the scrub fields
and the shining flies, the many-coloured, in the weed tips
and at night in the black cell
until silenced he beats on the improvised guitar
and growls the cry that comes from the broken rocks,
broken by the hammer, broken by the light,
and that comes from the sparkling rapids in the bird's throat:

the two sources:

all the damage, all the guilt,
yesterday and yesterday and yesterday,
tomorrow and tomorrow,
the splendour.

I often think back to that city of slim cones,
like an immense candle mould turned face down in the sand.
To those towers without entrances, hollow or solid within,
and the incomprehensible, vanished people.

Maybe I only dreamed they were made of some strange metal
under the dust or sand that clung to them.

Maybe they were only the petrified mounds
of a colony of termites, the little animals long ago released
from their slavery of being
one-note computers in wagons of chitin.

The city without a square
because nothing any longer needed to be discussed and
    decided.

Without a wall or a steeple with a clock
because the people themselves had become the clock.

The wanderer in a breath
builds a city of words
for delight and it shows
the other city its shame.
This city won't understand
but could. The words are hard
but only in calling it
to its intelligence.

The wanderer walks
out and away. The perilous
desert is a garden
even as it burns: the wanderer
admires the spring of diamond
flowers around his feet and knows
it equally flows around the feet of all
those sleeping in
the other city.

From it the wanderer
and the city of words
pass farther away and at night
they go out in sleep.
In that common gift
they wait for the common
splendour of day. The sharp
cones of the city back there
where the citizens rest
upright, contained,

dropping behind him
rise ever sharper
within him in the dark.

At each step — breaths
are the steps — the wanderer
begins and finishes
the journey. In every step
in the daytime where breath
hurts as the heart trudges
toward failure. In every breath
at night where the steps,
ongoing in the muscles,
are taken into sleep
and the unforeseeable
day of dreams.

You had nothing to live for there.
Only life. But where is there that life can't be sung
and what other task of life exists but singing?

Where is there that life can't be sung?
Only in the bed of final pain
and the bed of wandering.
There restlessness and tiredness preoccupy the traveller,
mirages and the stones and hope of arrival
continuously annoy and distract.

There
there is not a single leaf,
there is not a moment to see a leaf.

Another oasis. High reeds and trees like sprays of feathers.
The ground blocked from our sight by so much greenery,
despite our elevation on the inches of a dune.
But a glimpse shone through, a spark, the sparkling
of water flowing there. We descended
and entering found the lepers
behind each clump, lying in every fold of earth.
The spores of their disease drifted along,
the stream's surface was dusty and thick with them,
trapping the water striders. We fled.

Another oasis. A breath of freshness. Mud-brick huts clustered
in the palm grove. We descended. In each doorway
people lolled and twitched, twisted up
to child sizes and terrifying shapes.

Another oasis . . . like the others, almost silent,
and in our memory as we struggled away
filled with howling. After each one,
the youngest who had remained to us
was found missing.
We went searching for him among our various parties.
But he'd stayed behind.

The youngest among us: it wasn't that he hated us
with our grey, pitted bodies, hated us
from his transparent slenderness
of a summer grass blade or curve of falling water.

We were his apprenticeship in the desert,
but with us in the desert he was an orphan.
How could he have stayed any longer? He belonged
with the green places and the huts and their human decay
and at their ending the valley of the ashes.

We wanted to shout that we were miserable too
but it seemed clear he couldn't hear us.
We weren't broken and alone enough.

Which is more silent —
the full tomb sealed
or the empty tomb's gape
after its word has left?

VIII

When night begins to come, in the violet black,
we eat in silence. Whatever glow remains
suffuses the black dirt roads on thick knuckles
of broad thumbs clutching chunks of bread
and dipping in the stew. The wide, cracked lips tremor,
pressing together, as the jaws work.

We take our pattern from our animals. Unpacked, unsaddled,
they stand near each other, not very near,
or others nose to nose, or at inexplicable angles,
sometimes chewing, sometimes waiting, sometimes sleeping.
Sometimes a snort in the quiet.

When we write our logs
of the day's progress, the words take these patterns
of the mute, isolated animals born to flocks.

The stars are chips of ice.
Down here, no light.
But there must be light underneath some unseeable horizon
that shines upward and makes them glint,
inhabiting them.

I'd like, I do like, to say we,
but can't believe it.
No one can speak for another man or woman.
That would be to dream the time of myth,
when a whole people journeyed as one person, seeking a
    home —
Three years we travelled — or a meaning, as they used to say.
They used to use those words indifferently: home, meaning.
Even in pain and sorrow on the sea, in their song of
    complaint,
there were these things they possessed without noticing.
They agreed. How rich they were. Though nothing
agreeable, it appears, existed
in their condition, living with animals, cheek
by jowl with the filth of cattle.

I'd like to say the stars shine with their own light.
And that like them, these people in the camp with me
shine from within. I'd like to say we. That we don't need
    the sun
to be redeemed from darkness, like the lizards do
that can't move when the light and heat of day end.

To say that the stars see the embers of our fires
as we see their constellations: unreadable
script of light that may be no script
yet raises in us the endless struggle to read.

I'd like to say our bodies shine
and the sun is only our emblem. But we forgot ourselves
and gave our light away
to a chip of ice.

As long as this lasts, this waking night, you start to feel
    your face
not an affront but the inevitable
stamped on a certain material.

It's never clear but you move toward it.

This feigning
one day will enter really into its ugliness
as into a great city through a gate at dawn.

And the rift will be healed or sealed
between aspiration, delusion, and your body.

Singing to my pillow. The boys used to laugh and throw
stones at the young old man dressed in mourning
who'd ride out of town each day on a donkey
that had the air of a sheep. You'd see him adrift
in the children's cemetery: untended markers,
blooming yellow weeds, butterflies,
feathery new acacia leaves, light like torn lace.

Or adrift in the lanes, watching the cigar maker,
blacksmith, fishmonger. Or at the locked park gate at night,
trying to see the ghosts or women in the fountain,
seeing the moonlight in its diamond thread, the few
lights down in the black valley. Hearing a dog bark far off.

Or in the fields with the spring oxen and autumn reapers.

He was happy in himself. He was sad and alone
in the others. They loved the songs he sang,
like their childhood songs, so old, and they sang them too
and despised his aloneness. To be alone is sadness,
the failed, the less than human, and they despised
their sadness, and caressed it in his songs, compelled
to love it there. And in this way they were together.

A relief that in this night, blackly glimmering sand,
there's nothing that reflects, no book that can be read,
no look that can be seen, no mirroring pool.

Here and now you slowly have to recognize,
slowly accept. No models here,
nothing to reply to, imitate, or scorn.
You have to produce your own style or faith.

Have to imagine your own face.
Only your hands can help a little. Only your tongue
muttering to its own ears
out of memory's fund. Your childhood and adolescence
refined to gaping shadows sketched on the dark.

There's nothing I understand,
nothing I can imagine,

but when you speak,
whether out into the air hoping
for someone to be there
now or someday,

or with someone you know and I overhear,

or when it seems you speak with me . . .

these times when your speaking becomes
talking together,

this I understand. Not well, it's true, not wholly,
not with my life and body,
but I understand a little. And yes,
with the leaning called yearning,
leaning toward you to hear better
with my life and body.

Did you hear me?
Your hair fell across your eyes, grey-green, grey-blue,
quietly considering, so what I said
plunged into you like a river at the waterfall,
pure and powerful in its inconsequence,
never reaching anything, sparkling in the quiet of the forest.

Did you hear me? I told you everything
into the silence of the sounds of emptiness around the house.
Hissing. Stirring of birds and snakes. Far-off thunder.
Your accompaniment.

I told you everything and felt you watching
my work, my house, the wide disc of the country.
I felt you seeing everything I did,
listening to everything I said,
but I didn't think you heard me.

I write you letters all night in my head.
Do you receive them? It seems the replies I hear,
that now you love me, you always loved me,
are a tinsel part I write for you and pronounce
in place of the great dramatist. His work,
the words he'd give you, would be hard amid the humour,
the cruelty — man, a being possessed by a living dagger,
    the cross —
the pratfalls, drunken servants, mangled language,
the catastrophic misunderstandings, accidents, and lies.
Especially the lies a man tells himself
and scarcely knows he tells, writing to a lost love,
cantar a la almohadilla, as the Spanish say,
lines never set down, forgotten as soon as formed,
repeated no doubt every night, while everyone is sleeping.

Yet you answer and say what I don't want to hear,
could not imagine. "Love, I was never to have children,
my womb was broken. I was right to pull away
and you went walking through the world and I
remembered you. That way you taught me: restlessness,
always insisting, though hard and frightened. If I went
    further,
you were my light, my first light till I found my own.
Now all of this has been . . . I can't say as it had to be
or should have been . . . but good. You're better alone.
And you were never alone. That was in a dream you have
    of me.
Forget it. Remember me. Talk to me every night."

We're far apart although together.
I talk to you silently in mind and see you
listening to me beyond the curvature of the earth,
answering me.

How did I dream such a thing?
I belong to a time before the idea of the sphere.
I belong to a people that knows dirt, not the planet.

Still, I've imagined it.
All I know is my longing that the earth be
the stream and banks of childhood
and still I'm filled with vastness, separation.

Then isn't empty vastness my own creation
in evil dreams? Unless you come here
and tell it with me, there is no true history. Just a man
who wonders by himself till time makes him a mummy.

At night the desert's vastness becomes mere knowledge.
All that can be seen and felt is the dark.
The dark, called vast, is small, a space as close as a hood,
as the earth to a face face down. A face maybe savouring,
greeting, and kissing. A face dying or dead, crying, asleep.

If there was ever vastness, it can't be seen or felt.
It turns to a memory, an idea.
It echoes awhile in thought but soon sleep comes.
The feet are stopped. Movement survives as the heart,
plodding onward into what was not until it came.
Sleep is the dark again in a new form
that wraps the body tighter and in it dreams
are a vast swarming world, a little town and farm
long bygone set in a legend in flower.

IX

The idea of a form releases water in me.

Mother, sister, lover: Earth,
some power has erased my mind,
repeat my curse and blessing,
let me remember. Let me know again
as when I was a child.

The idea of a form releases water in me.
The idea of your form. Shape of fountain and current.

Now I can see the desert plainly: no desert but a drought.
Earth between two moments of rain.
A life between two moments of life.

The zones that peace and justice once marked out
in the sheltering wild,
the zones that gracious streams used to establish
are given here as shadows: scorched arroyos
and slow sidewinding snakes of dune crests
with no life, moved by the wind.

It's better to know the dry expanse
as the long journey
between the shaded east and the mysterious western forests.
Better than to know it as the time remaining
after two gardens, two dreams,
a maybe once and a maybe.

Better to know every step like this
for the place the long journey
begins and ends.

Mother, sister, lover: Earth,
was it you who led me out that day
(and led me out every day
and still leads me out every day)
into your body?

That early morning the happy sparrow flock
of the other children was nowhere near
and I went out to the hill and the shade of the apple tree
    on the slope.

Below, the woods along your stream curved subtly
north and south, and in the hills beyond
a trestle flew and carried a stretch of rails
sparkling to where it soon was lost behind green shaggy
    ridges.
Here and there the grey ellipse of a water tower
or a four-toothed comb of black smokestacks,
a silver silo, a red barn, and on the river of highway
flowing upward to the crest, a long white truck
or the dot of a blue car: tiny beetles
crawling noiselessly. Mounting easily: angels.

"This is what I choose." Misery, anger: a cry.
And the glory of light that suspended that world
had stretched my chest and neck and pried

my jaw open. Did it want to separate mandible from skull and accomplish the long action of death in a second?

"This should be forever. If it has to go, then I'll go too, go with it. I love it. Why do you make it so that it all has to go away? I hate you. I love this place. I side with this. Kill me."

Five or six years old. "I side with this."
A choice in the body. Nearness
of a new love to the new
tearing in me. Nearness
as of a lover fused with me.
In the torn-open heart, a prophecy
of she who would come.
A girl: knowledge of her
when I did not know her
but with me she was growing up
beyond the hills I saw,
on their far side, in fields
the mirrors, the sisters of my own.

Mother, sister, lover: Earth,
was my cry your cry
against your death? Or are you
too wise for that in your constant
suffering and upthrust
of fountains?

Nymph, in thy orison,
my origin. With you I flowed
down with the river, swam
with the pickerel in the reeds,
flowered with lilies,
and reflected, reflected
light up into
the oaks and willows.

After the cry I looked up into the sky
and was calm again, everything was calm,
the sun was in my hair and in the purring
of my nerves at the base of the skull
and in the leaves of the tree and their rustling.

"Sun, I love you, your passing into night,

and night, I love you. I side with you.

But beyond you, night and day,
there's something that I hate."

Not many days later — my chastisement? — I woke up
in the night, choking as if struck in the throat. You, Earth,
were gone and a thought filled the black room:
my mother too, my father too, will die. And I vibrated,
turning and turning for a way out,
till dawn began and I got up and slipped away
from my quiet house while everyone was sleeping.

I went to the apple tree,
this time in the cold dew. The invisible low sun
threw the slim cones of the fir trees' elongated shadows
into the grey mist. And I watched exhausted
and listless, while the force
of misery was regathering unnoticed
under my wandering but exact attention
to everything I saw. Till bursting up
from God knows where, defiance
rose again and I shouted. I side with this. Let me die.
     But soon
calmed down again. Dawn had changed
to sunrise and the sun, strengthening,
drenched my head and nape and made
my nerves purr. There was silence otherwise,
the green splendour and the dew
were deserted, no children anywhere, the distant house fronts
all shut up with lightlessness except the glinting
of the slant sun along the streets, between the trees,
and I went home and slipped back into
my quiet house, where everyone was sleeping.

Despite the crowd of everyone who was, is, will be, and should
   have been that went along with us,

it was easy to be alone again, by myself in those wildernesses
   of childhood we were passing through, endless stretches of
   woods, rivers and streams, parkland, plains and fields,

and it was easy to be alone with you in those sites of our love.

It was not even strange that, long erased, that world was
   sparkling with a newness it had once possessed but had
   never possessed.

How was it that all of us, a mob that would more than cover
   and ruin many earths, went along agilely as if we were just
   one person? And as if we were two?

"Isn't this only a vision you've made from a wish, the sole
   salve for a wound like yours?" said someone next to me.
   You were next to me, but this voice was not you.

I answered no, I'm dead. I've always been dead
and a dead man can't wish. He's solely
his body, his being moved, a body in the dust
and wind, like water.

But how was it we talked
as if it were one person thinking, and we moved
as though we were one and also as though
we were now two? And as if we were four
since now we two had a daughter and son.
And we were eight, because another four
had to appear to let the son and daughter
love and mate. And we were sixteen
because that is almost the divine age, seventeen, and because
the sons and daughters had given birth. We were raised
remorselessly to all powers
and became as many as the final number
of what only grows and never is whole
and looks out from its advancing edge
at nothing, at the fountain. We moved along as one.
 We'd arrived
at a new, an adequate journey, a search
through the place to be found. The beauty,
the nonsense, and the law of mathematics
that had overshadowed us was in us now.

The man's uncleanness,
and the killing of the child.

The spring in the forest
where the madman and the murdered girl
once went, each alone, in their own times, to find
shade from the city, the desert of insistence.
To drink the silence of God.

The public fountain turned on again at last
in the beautiful square
this first warm day of a late spring.

The few things
or the one thing we seem to know.

Under green trees far away
the splendour, the light over everything,
fills with shadows,
a voice, a gesture
answering another, excited hands and eyes
finding themselves
living.

These dead, who invented only death.

Far away under green trees what was hidden
in the folds of clothing, crotch, and brain glows
in faces of an unruined adolescence.

The world came to me
in a long unbeginning and unending undulation
of sweetness enclosing everything.

Then I met you and saw my childhood
had been your body.

Next I learned your body is
a heap of heaps of sand, a collision,
accidents, a collection, a gulf of gulfs.

Then all these kissed me in your voice
and the only nothing
was when you took yourself away.

The darkness where a man falls forever
in your sex was the cave
that gave the adventurer an uncontrollable gift.

It spoke, walked, walked away, and held the horror
of the earth in your beauty again.

When the one speaking dies,
the widowed one remains.
This we know well, we see it habitually.
The widowed one remains
speaking the absence,
the dead one as if she never was,
she is still to come,
speaking the ordered chaos
of the whirling of the stones,
stones that shiver like leaves,
leaves that fall and blow along like stars,
stars that pass away like monsters,
monsters that turn to nothing
as heroes and goddesses do. All this
is the love song of the widowed one,
a moment ago conversation,
the belovèd.

An accidental structure:
she like you
could not have been,
but there was in an instant
the tying of a knot
in all the threads
of all the things: a knot
like a purple iris
tied in the highways,
the wars, desertifications,
the ripening wheat
around our homes
and the fireflies
in the blue-gold seeds,
the demolishing
collision of worlds,
the drawings away,
losses in the dark,
misery of childhood
in the poor house filled
with shouts and insects,
and then the new
moon of August — in all
threads of all things
a sudden knot, a
flower that speaks,
moves and dies
and came to meet me.

The wanderer prefers to know he is lost
to the other way of seeing:
that it's the earth that wanders lost in him.
That he is its desert.
That it is searching in him
maybe for nothing
to be found there, in such barrenness.

That the earth stumbles in him along what's called
a line or path but is
a tightening spiral:
horror of the circle joined
with the nonsense of lessening.

It's the earth that seeks some way through him.

It's the earth that in the still expanse he is
hopes to see something from the rise of the next dune.

On the long journey it is possible
to discover just one thing:
as you are to her, she is
a small being entrusted to your care.

And the one thing has its lemma.
Your care, rising to fury in desire,
lacks power. The adequate
care cannot be yours.

Every body broken. This
is hard to admit. Open the door. Admit
the bleeding stranger. Else
there never will be anyone with you in your house. This
is the only one there is.

This is your pounding, this is you
pounding, whining, cadging
to be admitted. Or lying,
lying there, a silence almost still,
with no word anymore except your body,
so that if no one will see
in your body what you're saying,
you'll never say anything again.

The light
that burns me up without wounding me

                              (I looked
into my deepest cut and saw your splendour)

making my body my body and
a form in transparency: shape
                              that finally gives
the reason for being of shape:

is this because the light loves the body?
It says love in me
so that I can understand me.

Understand me
as I die here, song
emanating in aloneness
in the imagination of a death in the desert,
my death, my imagination, in my room. Here
the window of my vision of the street
is draped in its flowing current, a curtain white and green,
apple flowers and leaves. They blow and sway
around the opened square of space I look through and
      are locks
around your face, so the air
entering my room, my death, my song
may be your voice.

Attainment is to be with someone
and it has no monument or prize.
It's to take nothing and set off into a vast land
beyond the sight of everyone,
leaving a ghost of yourself where you were
so that in seeing you they forget you
and don't know what you're doing.
It's to walk slowly into a vast land
uninhabited and maybe never to be inhabited
that begins to flower or will never flower.

In saying this I've produced my monument and prize.
Even the unstructured simplicity of the phrases
appears as art in this time when wisps of smoke of breath
are praised above the ode
and music's the stutter of the street
and the air filling and emptying at no intervals
with helicopters carrying the injured from the highway.

Let the word be only truth. The truth is
that nothing should be said of this. I couldn't resist
a monument, and like everything that might have not existed
now it's necessary, it has its place and use,
but my monument is a ghost and the prize of my ghost and
I am elsewhere,
lost and hidden in her.

Every step was into a new world
drenched in memory and longing: these were the dew there.
The sun sparkled in it, the low sun
that pierced the tips of the oak crowns
on the eastern, the far-side banks. A sparkling
that never would leave us, that later we'd know again
in the splendour of a breast shining in lace,
the stirring of birds by the creek,
the fluttering in our struck heart. The sun
shone through the drops of memory,
and the child was wet, chilled,
and warmed. The child we were.
He and she purred in nerves and muscles
and brought their eyes close to the places
they could see in the drops, some of the new worlds
of the place where we'd halted for the morning.

Summer solstice: the fixed idea
of the sun, fixed
in idea only while the sun
is eating itself, burning itself for fuel against the cold
(how long can it continue
to draw all life out of itself
with no companion to solace it, no world?)
as it goes on wandering
in blackness. The sun still
this mild day this June in the

light wind
so beautiful to listen to
in the trees. Not over the bare
ground pounded to powder, a howl
or a moan. In the trees
and across the crops and around
the balconies and open windows,
the blowing white curtains of the house, how good,

how good a child
to get up in the room up in the maple crowns,
in the second story, an ark come
to rest as the waters of night receded,
come to rest in the silver maple boughs . . .

a child in the music of the billowing
curtains, the unknowable
rhythm of the quiet click of the curtain hooks in the

light wind,
how good a child
to get up with the sun to begin
our wandering anew.

Sequence is in the tradition of the sequential poem, often seen as the characteristic long poem of our times. It uses the two foundational modern sequences, *In Memoriam* and *Song of Myself,* as well as early precedents that these sometimes acknowledge (e.g., Shakespeare's sonnets), and many examples written since the 1850s. I wish to mention two in particular, Seferis's *Mythistorema* (trans. Rex Warner; trans. Edmund Keeley and Philip Sherrard) and Lagerkvist's *Evening Land* (trans. W. H. Auden and Leif Sjöberg). Also important was *Exaltación de la luz (Exaltation of Light)* by Homero Aridjis (trans. Eliot Weinberger). The following notes are meant simply to credit direct borrowings, not to identify all the many instances, perhaps visible and useful only to me, of the presence of books and poems.

P. 9 *"The music of the night,"* . . . : The two quoted passages are translations of haiku-like poems by Homero Aridjis ("Romántica," "Romantic," from *Vivir para ver / Living to See*) and Octavio Paz ("Aparición," "Apparition," from *Ladera este / East Face*).

P. 12 *The caravans of the merchants* . . . : ll. 1–2. The translated line is by José Ángel Valente from "La Mañana" ("Morning") in *Poemas a Lázaro* (1960); there's a text and a translation of it in *Landscape with Yellow Birds: Selected Poems by José Ángel Valente,* trans. Thomas Christensen; 26–9. The image by Anaïs Nin is from *A Spy in the House of Love.* The image from Jiménez's childhood comes from an autobiographical writing that can be found in various compilations and is quoted in several biographies.

P. 14 *When the heel strikes* . . . : l. 7: "anywhere out of here" is from
Baudelaire's "Any Where Out of the World" in *Le spleen de
Paris*. The title is in English in the original. The poem
begins, "Life is a hospital where every patient is obsessed
with the desire of changing beds" (trans. Louise Varèse).

P. 21 *O the magnificence of* . . . : ll. 3–5: "Following Barth and
others, I have often recalled that glory is revelation. God
glorifies himself when he reveals himself as he is . . . We
ourselves are called upon to be the glory of God . . ." Ellul,
The Subversion of Christianity (trans. Geoffrey W.
Bromiley), 76. The idea that glory is revelation, the
uncovering of the essential fact, operates throughout the
poem, including in the word *splendour*.

Another source for this is the work of Octavio Paz,
which frequently uses the word and concept *splendour* as
revelation of both the nourishing and the troubling aspects
of the world: ("the world / is the cleft the splendor the
whirl," *Blanco*; "splendor unsheathed, the reflections from
an empty can — high on a pyramid of scraps — pierce
every point of space," "Plain") (trans. Eliot Weinberger,
The Poems of Octavio Paz).

Also important to me is Guillermo Sucre's phrase from
an essay on Paz, "un estado de continua metamorfosis de
lo real, que pierde su opacidad y se vuelve verdaderamente
real, esplendor material" ("a state of continuous
metamorphosis of the real, which loses its opacity and
becomes *real* indeed: material splendour") ("La fijeza y el
vértigo" in *Octavio Paz: El escritor y la crítica*, ed. Pere
Gimferrer, 48).

P. 22 *Who traced a finger* . . . : l. 2. refers to Breton, *L'air de
l'eau*, part 13: "On me dit que là-bas les plages sont noires /
De la lave allée à la mer / Et se déroulent au pied d'un
immense pic fumant de neige / Sous un second soleil de

150

serins sauvages . . ." It's Tenerife in the Canaries ("serins" means "canaries") that provides the image.

P. 23 *We set out because* . . . : l. 7: "For the figure of this world is passing away . . . ," a possible translation of part of 1 Corinthians. 7:31; cf. Giorgio Agamben, *The Time That Remains* (trans. Patricia Dailey).

P. 27 Commedia *without an end* . . . : The idea of "the marriage bed of yes and no" recalls Octavio Paz, who says something similar in several ways in various poems, e.g., "No and Yes / together / two syllables in love," *Blanco* (trans. Eliot Weinberger).

P. 33 Part III: The details of this section are from my experience, but the plot comes from a brief background incident in *Jude the Obscure*, though finally I changed it almost beyond recognition: "Well — that tale, ye know; he that was gibbeted just on the brow of the hill by the Brown House. . . . She ran away from him, with their child, to her friends; and while she was there the child died. He wanted the body, to bury it where his people lay, but she wouldn't give it up. Her husband then came in the night with a cart, and broke into the house to steal the coffin away; but he was catched, and being obstinate, wouldn't tell what he broke in for. They brought it in burglary, and that's why he was hanged and gibbeted on Brown House Hill. His wife went mad after he was dead" (Norton Critical Edition, 223).

P. 38 *They were the law there* . . . : The italicized lines come from a Catholic song we sang in May crownings when I was a child. The song, generally called "Bring Flowers of the Rarest," from its first line, has lyrics attributed to Mary E. Walsh and a tune of apparently unknown origin. It appeared at least as early as 1885, in the hymnal *Laudis Corona: The New Sunday School Hymn Book* . . . (Hymnary.org).

P. 49 *When time will be restored* . . . : "forever arriving" is Eliot Weinberger's translation of "y llega siempre," l. 6 of *Piedra de sol* (*Sunstone*) by Octavio Paz; Paz repeats the line as his poem's last.

P. 53 *The freedom that is god* . . . : "Freedom, for which fire became man" is from Breton, *L'air de l'eau,* part 5: "En toute liberté / Cette liberté / Pour laquelle le feu même s'est fait homme."

P. 54 *What did you go out* . . . : Matthew 7:11 and Luke 7:24, "What did you come out into the desert to see?" (trans. Richmond Lattimore); this appears several more times in *Sequence.*

P. 55 *The sufficient illusion* . . . : ll. 6–8, "the building / becomes, returns to / being growing" is a concept and image drawn from Blaise Moritz, *Crown and Ribs*; for instance, "Perhaps construction is near to me, / but like root and stem and leaf, like bone and flesh, // I'd want to grow it for you, patient now in our ruin / of cement and brick . . ." ("The Builder") and "the humility of some famous landscape architect . . . / to think of creating something that requires the collaboration of plants, and time / beyond your own life, such that the beauty fulfilled can only be for others" ("At the Offices of the Perishable Press").

P. 56 *You heard a murmuring* . . . : Stanzas 2 through 4 of this poem are a collage of paraphrased phrases from Jeremiah 30 and 31. The murmuring and babble of the prophetic stream is from Vergil, *Aeneid* VII 83–4, where King Latinus, to consult the oracle of his father, the prophetic god Faunus, goes into the forest, which "sacro / fonte sonat," "sounded with the sacred spring."

P. 57 *To be grateful to time* . . . : The phrase "Time is the mercy of Eternity" is from Blake, *Milton,* copy D, plate 24, line 72.

The lines continue, "without Times swiftness / Which is the swiftest of all things: all were eternal torment . . . "

P. 63 *If you ever stop or slow* . . . : "the garden in future merging into the wild" is one of the concepts of Wordsworth's "The Ruined Cottage."

". . . a ship you once hailed for rescue / and it passed by unseeing": Géricault's painting *The Raft of the Medusa*.

P. 66 *They walked and walked* . . . : This poem is a translation, or perhaps, given the expansions and additions, a paraphrase of the first sentence of *Dr. Zhivago*; it incorporates information from the third paragraph. The last two lines are derived from the last line of *Song of Myself*, "I stop somewhere waiting for you," in such a way as to retain its primary meaning but bring out its recessive one.

P. 70 *What did you come out* . . . : l. 11, "all the house behind me sleeping," which is repeated with slight variations several times in *Sequence*, is a paraphrase of San Juan de la Cruz, "La noche oscura" ("The dark night"), ll. 4–5: "salí sin ser notada, / estando ya mi casa sosegada" ("I went out unnoticed, / all my house being then asleep").

P. 75 *Still another retelling* . . . : The appearance of Ulysses, which consists of this and the next five pages, refers to "Ulysses" in *Zeppelin*, Blaise Moritz, which in turn refers to Tennyson's "Ulysses." Elpenor is important in the poetry of Seferis.

P. 81 *To be on the road* . . . : The introductory phrase, of course, recalls Jack Kerouac.

P. 82 *The lonely public road. No one* . . . : This opening phrase recalls Wordsworth, his early poem of the impoverished demobbed soldier, "a desolation, a simplicity," who lingers "in the public ways," on "the road's watery surface" (incorporated in *The Prelude*, fourteen-book version, Book Fourth, ll. 370–469).

p. 83 *The lonely public road* . . . : The phrase "the spring in the forest," which is repeated elsewhere in *Sequence*, is from Trakl's "De Profundis": "Gottes Schweigen / Trank ich aus dem Brunnen des Hains" ("The silence of God / I drank from the spring in the forest").

p. 87 *We yearned for* . . . : The phrase "the everlasting / arrogance of eminent persons" is from Whitman, I feel certain, but I cannot now find it.

p. 88 *We yearned to grow* . . . : "possess it merely": *Hamlet*, act I, scene ii: "things rank and gross in nature / Possess it merely," "merely" meaning "entirely." ll. 18–23 are paraphrased from Whitman's "A Song of Joys." The final three lines are Luke 6:24: "But woe to you that are rich: for you have your consolation" (Douay-Rheims).

p. 94 *You had nothing to live for there* . . . : The use of "hard labour" here was suggested by William Arrowsmith's use of this phrase to translate Pavese's title *Lavorare stanca*, thus bringing the English-language meaning of a prison sentence into Pavese's "stubborn work."

p. 96 *The wanderer in a breath* . . . : "The perilous / desert is a garden" refers to Blake, "The Argument," in *The Marriage of Heaven and Hell*: ". . . in a perilous path / The just man kept his course along / The vale of death. / Roses are planted where thorns grow. / And on the barren heath / Sing the honey bees."

"In that common gift / they wait for the common / splendour of day" refers to Wordsworth, *The Excursion*, l. 754 ff.: "— Beauty — a living presence of the Earth, / Surpassing the most fair ideal forms . . . // Paradise, and groves / Elysian, Fortunate Fields . . . // . . . the discerning intellect of Man, / When wedded to this goodly universe / In love and holy passion, shall find these / A simple produce of the common day."

"At each step": The idea that every step contains a whole journey is informed by Blake, e.g., *Milton*: "Every Time less than a pulsation of the artery / Is equal in its period & value to Six Thousand Years. / For in this Period the Poets Work is Done: and all the Great / Events of Time start forth & are concievd in such a Period / Within a Moment . . ." (Copy D, plate 28, l. 62 – plate 29, l. 3). This is repeated later in *Sequence*, e.g., in the second poem beginning *The idea of a form*. . . . For me this concept comes equally from Blaise Moritz, "A Day's Work, a Lifetime" (*Crown and Ribs*): the title, the entire sequence, and such passages as "There's a day's work, a lifetime / in the next small movement / of my new and unearthly foot."

p. 99 *Another oasis* . . . : l. 4, "the youngest," see Seferis, *Mythistorema* 12, "The youngest won it and disappeared" (trans. Edmund Keeley and Philip Sherrard).

p. 106 *The stars are chips of ice.* . . . : The italicized line is my false memory of l. 2 of Seferis's *Mythistorema* in the Keeley and Sherrard translation, which turns out to be in fact "three years we waited intently . . ."

p. 109 *Singing to my pillow* . . . : The poet pictured is Juan Ramón Jiménez as he presents himself in his *Platero y yo*. Some of the imagery comes from other Jiménez poems: "Primavera amarilla" ("Yellow Spring"), "Viene una música lánguida . . ." ("There Comes a Languid Music . . .") and "Octubre" ("October").

p. 120 *Mother, sister, lover: Earth* . . . : Tennyson, "Oenone": "O mother, hear me yet before I die. / Hear me, O earth" (ll. 252–3). Shelley, *Prometheus Unbound*, Act I passim; e.g., "The curse / Once breathed on thee [Jupiter] I would recall. . . ." and "Venerable Mother! / All else who live and suffer take from thee [Earth] / Some comfort: flowers and fruit, and happy sounds, / And love, though fleeting; these may not be mine. / But mine own words, I pray, deny me not" (ll. 58–9, 186–90).

P. 121 *The idea of a form* . . . : The common phrase "the long journey" (which is repeated in *On the long journey it is possible* . . .) comes, for me, from Seferis's "Stratis Thalassinos Among the Agapanthi": "The first thing God made is love . . . // The first thing God made is the long journey . . ." (trans. Keeley and Sherrard).

P. 122 *Mother, sister, lover: Earth* . . . : the first stanza draws on Whitman, "There Was a Child Went Forth."

P. 124 *Five or six years old* . . . : "Nymph, in thy orison" is *Hamlet*, act III, scene i, immediately after the "To be or not to be" speech. Hamlet calls out to Ophelia, "Nymph, in thy orisons / Be all my sins remembered."

P. 126 *Not many days later* . . . : The concluding phrase, "and slipped away / from my quiet house while everyone was sleeping," is another of the references to San Juan de la Cruz, "La noche oscura" ("The dark night"), mentioned above, as is the final line of the next poem, *I went to the apple tree* . . .

P. 133 *The man's uncleanness* . . . : Stanza 2 refers again to Trakl's "De Profundis."

P. 142 *The light / that burns me* . . . : The phrase "a death in the desert" is the title of a poem by Robert Browning.

P. 144 *Every step was into* . . . : The phrase "the eastern, the far-side, banks" recalls Terry Smith's song "Far-Side Banks of Jordan."

P. 145 *Summer solstice: the fixed idea* . . . : Octavio Paz, "Solo a dos voces" ("Solo for Two Voices"): "Winter solstice: / sun stopped, / world wandering. / Sun in exile, / fixity at white heat. / The black white earth, / asleep, / flung on itself, / is a fallen stone . . ." (trans. John Frederick Nims).

My sincere thanks go to everyone who helped me in the writing and preparation of *Sequence*. To Sue Sinclair, my editor for the book, who made many suggestions that improved wording, clarity, and organization. To T, and to Roseanne Carrara, for essential discussion, and to Blaise Moritz, for our ongoing dialogue in conversation and in poetry. To Jan Zwicky, for discussion and for a crucial hint. To Damian Rogers, friend, poet, and poetry editor of Anansi, for her enthusiasm toward the book and her consistently helpful attention to its development. To Stuart Ross and Peter Norman, whose alert, sensitive copy editing and proof reading added improvements and prevented errors. To Kelly Joseph, managing editor, for smoothly coordinating the complex editing job and providing many good ideas. To Sarah MacLachlan, Janie, Matt, Mark, and all at Anansi, whose help and friendship make it a cherished literary home for me.

A. F. Moritz has published seventeen books of poetry, as well as works of non-fiction and translation. He is the recipient of the Guggenheim Fellowship, the Ingram Merrill Fellowship, the Award in Literature of the American Academy of Arts and Letters, selection to the Princeton Series of Contemporary Poets, and the Bess Hokin Prize of *Poetry* magazine. His collection *The Sentinel* won the 2009 Griffin Poetry Prize, and his *The New Measures* received the Raymond Souster Award. He lives in Toronto.